ONE WHOLE NAKED ME

ALSO BY FREDERICK ESPIRITU

THE PATH TO AWESOMENESS

ONE WHOLE NAKED ME

FREDERICK ESPIRITU

One Whole Naked Me
The Poetry of Awesomeness

Copyright © 2016 by Frederick Espiritu

All rights reserved. No part of this publication may be reproduced, except for brief quotations, without the prior permission of the copyright owner of this publication.

Printed by Kindle Direct Publishing

First Edition

ISBN 978-621-8023-13-0

I remember now.
I've always loved poetry.

CONTENTS

BEAUTY

LOVE AT FIRST SIGHT	17
BLIND	18
I SEE	19
BACK TO BACK	20
A LETTER TO THE BELOVED	21
DEAR MOON	22
THE COUPLE	23
ECLIPSE	24
THE LOOK	25
SOAR	26
OPEN EYES	27
NIGHT SKY	28
SOUL DANCE	29
RETROGRADE	30
FEEL ME	31
INEFFABLE	32
UNCHARTED	33
NO REGRETS	34
A THOUSAND LIVES	35
BURNT	36
SHATTERED	37
DIVINE	38
SILENT ECHOES	39
MUSIC PLEASE	40
HORIZON	41

LOVELY NATURE	42
THE MAGICIAN	43
RESTART	45
FORGIVENESS	46
NEW WORLD	47
THE CHASE	48
TWIN	49
THIS	50
WARRIOR OF THE HEART	52
HOME	53

GOODNESS

ONE WHOLE NAKED ME	57
PERFECT	58
THE CANDIDATE	59
JAMES LOVE	60
LOVER OF LIFE	61
STARDOM	62
THE HEART OF IMAGINATION	63
THE MANUSCRIPT	64
CHANGE TOPIC	65
HI	66
THE MASTERPIECE	67
YOUR BOOK	68
OMNIPRESENCE	69
WINGS	70
DANCE	71
I LOVE YOU TOO, SUN	72
MEDI-DATE	73
THE ANSWER	74
LAST JUDGEMENT	75

HEAVEN ON EARTH	76
EARTH OF MINE	77
THE TOURIST	78
HAPPY BIRTHDAY	79
HONEYLOVE	80
HALLELUJAH	81
HEARTNAPPED	82
DAILY REMINDER	83
FAIRYTALE	84
DREAMS	85

TRUTH

YOUR HOME IS IN YOUR HEART	89
LIFE'S A FRIEND	91
GRATITUDE	92
THE VOICE	94
PURPOSE	95
FREE WILL	96
SCREAM	98
FREEDOM	99
PATIENCE	100
HEALING	101
POSITIVE	102
INNOCENCE	103
THE SCIENTIST	104
TRUE LOVE	105
CHANGELESS	106
HAPPINESS	107
LASTING BEAUTY	108
KINDNESS	109
GAME	110

TREASURE OF THE HEART	111
HIDE AND SEEK	112
WORDS	113
SELF-MASTERY	114
WARRIOR OF THE LIGHT	115
LOVE AND LIGHT	116
SOUL TO SOUL	117
STANDBY	118
FISH IN THE OCEAN	119
SOMEONE SOMEWHERE	120
CHALLENGE	122
CHANGE	123
MOTHER AND CHILD	125
TWIN FLAME	126
THE VOW	128

INTRODUCTION

Being a writer was the last thing I had imagined of myself becoming. Who would have thought that the kid who despised reading has turned out to be someone writing his own books? And I can't help but giggle whenever I'm reminded of all the book reports my sister lent me just so I can have something to submit for the school project requirements. Yes, I copied them all! What would you expect from someone who reads book cover AND cover? As in literally the front and back cover only.

I guess now the joke is on me. Nonetheless, it's for a good laugh. And laughter is always good. I wouldn't be as creative as I could if not for the touch of humor.

The gift has always been there. I just wasn't paying attention to it, much less to myself. I was busy pushing my way up the corporate ladder, seeking other opportunities to earn money, then quitting my job, and having high hopes I'd find success in entrepreneurship. And in those events that transpired in my life, writing has always been there. But it never really occurred to me to consider it as a gift.

It wasn't until I struck up a conversation with a friend and colleague, Joey Lee, about each other's greatest gift. He was quite certain about himself in the field of music. And indeed, he is one talented musician I know. As for me, I have often regarded myself as the *"jack of all trades, master of none"*. It was him who first gave me a sort of reassurance about my flair for writing.

Only then did I consciously assess myself for the latent talent I have. Many people have also given me credit for the inspiration they found in my writing. What if I was the only one left questioning my own potential? What did they see in me that must have been hidden in plain sight?

It's true. We hardly notice life's greatest treasure that has been lying all along beneath our feet. It seems like we came here forgetting that we brought something with us to offer to the world. Then, we go about in life thinking it's something we can find out there, so we search for it in all the wrong places.

In the stages of introspection, the journey to rediscovering myself led me to remembering that long-forgotten treasure. And what better way for life to reveal it than as a pre-birthday present in the year 2014. Next thing I know, I began writing a poem once again – *"A Letter to the Beloved"*. I mentioned 'again' because the last time I wrote prior to that was back in 2001, a tribute poem to my fellow graduating high school batch mates.

January of the following year, with no more than the intention of sharing and rekindling the passion for writing, I submitted a piece as an entry for a poetry contest held monthly on Goodreads. Then, an author and poet named Paul Morabito, happened to stumble upon it and got interested in publishing my poems for the poetry anthology he was working on at the time. My first few pieces eventually became part of the two volumes for that project series, entitled *"Mirrored Voices"*.

That milestone served as a springboard for me to leap toward my calling in life. And it was reaffirmed when a psychic friend I met did an impromptu intuitive reading based on one particular poem I wrote. She asserted that I came here for that calling - to write.

It was more of an icing on the cake. For I have already found within, at the core of my being, what makes me come alive.

Writing is a lot like falling in love.

Poetry is the art of doing it with words.

> *"The purpose of life is to discover your gift; the work of life is to develop it; and the meaning of life is to give your gift away."* — *David Viscott*

In my first book, *The Path to Awesomeness*, I shared an essay as my declaration of love for poetry. This is the testament to that. *One Whole Naked Me* is the gift I am now giving away.

I am all yours!

OWN Me.

BEAUTY

LOVE AT FIRST SIGHT

My heart and my soul are best of friends.
Inseparable, yet extreme opposite of each.
One's weakness is the other's strength.
From the bleeding to death
comes the breathing to life.

Pain gives birth to joy.
One moment you're broken.
The next, you're whole.
Painful, at the same time beautiful.

My heart and my soul are best of friends.
And their friendship started
the day you and I first met.

BLIND

I fell in love with a girl
who wears no make-up at all,
yet still can find herself
utterly beautiful.

                                                And here I go again,
                                                                falling.

I SEE

> In love, I see
> a thousand beautiful places.
> One glance at you
> and you already take me there.

You blinded me with your smile.
But the light inside your heart
made me see again.

BACK TO BACK

Love.

Such a word too often used
but too often mistaken.
Perhaps the world conspired
for something else to believe in.
Something to hold on to
while we're lost and seeking.

                                    Somehow,
                    between forgotten memories
                        and fading dreams,
          you and I managed to find our way.

                My joy back to your laughter.
                Your silence back to my peace.

I led myself back to love.
Then it was love, as always,
that keeps leading me back to you,
you to me,
us back to ourselves.

A LETTER TO THE BELOVED

Let me love you,
until you fall in love with yourself.

Let my light burn for you,
until you feel the warmth of your own flame.

Let me sing,
until you can hear your music.

My beloved,
for as long as you are dreaming
let me stay awake
until you, my true love,
are no longer asleep.

DEAR MOON

Go on.
I did not mean to interrupt you.
While I wait to catch your attention,
I can amuse myself talking to the moon
with all these words
I've been dying to tell you.

> *"Dear Moon,*
> *I love being your Sun.*
> *You could say I'm the reason why you shine.*
> *But I keep coming back everyday*
> *because I want to keep telling you*
> *that no matter what phase you take,*
> *you still are,*
> *and will always be*
> *the utmost reason why I burn."*

THE COUPLE

When it comes to True Love,
the Sun and the Moon
are a couple to be reckoned with.
From our perspective, they seem to be apart.
From theirs, they are inseparable.

                                    Being True Lovers,
                        they can settle for a few glances,
                    letting go without losing touch,
           holding on to the promise of Heaven
              that their longings will eventually
                    lead them back together.

The Sun and the Moon.
Two individuals sharing the same essence.
One says, *"I'll take care of you by day."*
The other, *"I'll watch over you by night."*
With that kind of love,
they light up the whole world.

                      That's the kind of couple we are.
                      You are that kind of Moon to me.
                 And I'm willing to burn all my life
                  just to be that kind of Sun to you.

ECLIPSE

I couldn't come any closer.
Maybe it's supposed to be this way.
The Sun was not always meant
to shine beside his Moon.

So as long as Heaven forbids our union,
I will bind myself to this poem.

Although my hands can't hold her,
at least,
these words can.

THE LOOK

There is something in your gaze
the way the verses of a poem
meet the melody of a song.
Like the rendezvous of the sun and the moon
exchanging vows with one another.

I often stare at the starlit skies
and wonder how they fit inside your eyes.
They open the gates of heavens
I can't help but be mesmerized.

I came from stormy seas
and many deserted islands.
But in knowing that love is in all places,
I have gone forth as a wanderer
in the hopes of one day
the winds will carry me home to you.

SOAR

I will let you go if,
and only if
you promise to spread your wings
and fly.

If one day
you find that the sky is too vast
and a lonesome place,
you can always return home
and find rest in my embrace.

I will mend whatever is broken,
grow your feathers back
so you can soar again.

                                        This time around,
                                               higher.

OPEN EYES

Someday, you're going to wake up
with eyes that see
how beautiful you already are
as you always were.

On that day,
you're going to realize
what I saw in you
from the very beginning.

It never faded away since then.

NIGHT SKY

Given the chance to lie awake
beneath the night sky,
I would prefer staring at the moon
and winking at the stars.
I would look for meteors and constellations.

Spare me tonight.
Let's pretend that your brilliance
is less irresistible to my sight.

For when I lay my eyes to rest,
in the midst of darkness,
once again,
I will be back to seeing you alone
and remain only in your light.

SOUL DANCE

In the stillness of the night,
the thought of you
leaves my mind
in quiet unrest
and moves my heart
in a delightful fashion,
tuning my soul
to the music
that makes it dance.

RETROGRADE

Could you recognize him
in times when he becomes a stranger to himself?
Would you take a closer look
if he reveals a marred reflection
of the image you had of who he is?

These are only few of the many hidden flaws
he's not proud of.

His fear is his imperfection.
At his weakest, he turns into a disaster.
And the thought of you
getting caught up in his storm
scares him the most.

He'd rather go away.
But if you knew the way where he can find rest,
would you take him there?
If you were the calmness to his rage,
the stillness to his thunder,
would you stay until he falls asleep?

Stay.
Because after the storm passes,
you are the first sunshine
he would love to see
when he wakes up.

FEEL ME

        I broke everything inside me
            that needs to be broken.

So when I finally give myself to you,
all you can experience
is no less than
the most pristine part
of my being.

INEFFABLE

Pardon my incessant stare.
My eyes were born of patience.
They have waited far too long
to behold the sight of you.

Don't get them wrong.
What they see is beyond the sense of seeing.
And as much as I want to put it into words,
I can't.
You are simply inexplicable.
Yet what you make me feel
explains everything I can't say.

UNCHARTED

I want to touch you
in the same way
a pen touches a paper
when I write a poem.

A poem, soul-deep romantic,
that I can reach
uncharted places inside you
using only words.

NO REGRETS

I never regret a moment
I spent being in love.
Perhaps, the only mistake
I cannot afford
is not spending those timeless
moments with you.

A THOUSAND LIVES

They say that lovers live a thousand lives
only to spend one last
with their beloved.

I can't remember how many I've had.
But none of them matter anymore.

You are worth all the breaths
love has taken away
from my entire existence.

BURNT

I burned myself ages ago.
What you see are merely dregs
and leftover ashes.

And you,
you my love,
are the other flame
that keeps me on fire.

SHATTERED

"How can you mend the pain?" you ask.

> To this my love I say to you,
> I did not come to make you whole.

> But with the slightest touch on your cheek,
> I will make every piece of you
> feel as though
> you were never broken.

DIVINE

Take me to the darkest chambers of your heart.
I will search for the light through your eyes,
taste eternity from your lips,
hold the heavens with your hands
and caress every fabric of your soul
like it was mine.

SILENT ECHOES

Let my words become a blanket
to comfort you in your suffering.
Wear this cloak to conceal the agony
as my lips make your wounds unscathed.

A drop of my blood
will stream down into your oceans grief.
And I will swim beyond the abyss of pains
to carry you back to the shore of relief.

For a moment,
rest your restless soul.

Now, hold my hands.
Watch as they turn into feathers
while I breathe the wind
beneath your wings.

Rise up my phoenix!
Emerge from your dusty old shadows.
Fly and soar high above the heavens.

Be the brightest of stars.
Let your radiance beam across the Universe.

When you do,
leave your ashes burning
as the silent echoes in my heart.

MUSIC PLEASE

They told us
love is only but a feeling.
I told them
love is what we are made of.

Don't bother an explanation.
I'm not asking for your cleverness.
What I long to hear is silence,
the empty spaces in between.

All I want is this music.
Her warm breath
that sends shiver to my skin.
And her voice
that keeps my heart beating.

HORIZON

I am your sky.

You are my ocean.

I look forward to meeting you
at the horizon.

LOVELY NATURE

I followed the hues forming in the skies.
You appeared on the other end of the rainbow.

When our paths crossed
I felt my heart fluttered.

For the very first time,
I learned how to fly.

THE MAGICIAN

I have tales of magic to tell.
And from you, I only ask one thing.
Listen.

Lend me your heart.
A shattered piece is all I need.
Have you seen a stone turn into diamond?
Pain scratches you to your elegance.

Don't be afraid, I will never fail you.
Fear disappears in my presence.
Whenever you are in attendance,
I become the greatest magician.

The fiercest lion is not in the wilderness.
It's in the cage sealed inside my chest.
The world held it in captivity.
You alone can set it free.

Close your eyes.
When you feel like falling, just let go.
My wings have been patiently waiting,
yearning for a single moment of our embrace.

Can you hear my soul sing?
Let this music unchain you.
They sound like symphony to the ears.
Make the stream of notes flow endlessly.

Now, for the grand majestic act,
I will whisper three words.
Just listen.
Silence will do the rest of the talking.

RESTART

From every ending
comes a new beginning.

Among them,
the beginning of you in me
is the one thing
I love to start
over and over again.

FORGIVENESS

For the man who,
in his own weakness,
has inflicted this pain
that sealed your bleeding heart.

                Allow me to speak on his behalf,

                        "I'm sorry."

                            Now let it go, my love,
                                for this is where
                                I intend to come in.

NEW WORLD

I woke up today
breathing a different air.
It's the fragrance of her soul
that forever lingers in my heart.

I was reborn with a new pair of eyes,
one that only sees her.
It's a whole new world
where love is all there is.

THE CHASE

Sometimes, just sometimes,
I want to hide myself from you
then seek you all over again.

That feeling.

>   Of getting lost
>   while going in the right direction;
>   Of falling
>   that takes you on a high;
>   Of reaching
>   for something that seems so far
>   yet so close within your grasp.

And of dying,
knowing that at any given time,
in an exceptional place,
I will find countless reasons to live again
for the one
who makes all the endless chase
worthwhile.

>   You.

TWIN

She is the exact replica of my soul,
the epitome of beauty in perfection.

Just looking at her makes me feel
like I'm the most beautiful man
who has ever set foot on earth.

THIS

Do you want to see
all the wrong things in our world?

        You sit right there.

                Then notice how many people
                move too fast about in life,
                they go blind over the miracle
                of being in the moment.

Now, do you want to see all the right things?

Well, I can't honestly speak for others.
But this is how it always works for me.
I just sit right here.

        Right here.
                Beside you.

Then silently,
I notice how all the wrong things in my world
just seem to start falling
into their rightful places.

        Right here.
                Beside you.

WARRIOR OF THE HEART

Courage brought me here.
I desperately tried to dress myself with words.
Yet excuses can no longer defend my walls.

So here I am.
Clueless.
Defenseless.
But I will tell you this,
for this is all you have to know.

I love you.

Nothing in this life
is more worth fighting for
than that.

HOME

My eyes saw her for the first time.
But her stance looks so familiar
like I've been staring at her
for as long as I can remember.

I was holding her hand
even before I touched it.
I was listening to her voice
even before I heard it.

Here she comes.

As she walks down the aisle,
I felt this presence inundated my soul.
A stirring sense of madness.
Intense unwavering silence.

She smiled.

In that very moment
I knew, at last,
I was home.

GOODNESS

ONE WHOLE NAKED ME

I'm setting a new fashion trend.
It's the most elegant
inexpensive way to be me.

*"To wear who I really am
or wear nothing at all."*

Now, that's a fashion statement!

PERFECT

Well, well, well.
Look who's here.

                                So,
                          is it my eyes,
                    or have you always been
                          this drop dead
                              perfect?

THE CANDIDATE

I have no clues
as to which comes faster.
The thoughts in my mind,
or the beating of my heart.
Either way, one thing is for sure.
Both are rushing towards you.

They were never like this before.
Who used to be on opposing sides
are now conjoined for the same advocacy:
"Make love, not war."

They have my full support.
No need for useless campaign and bribery.
When election comes,
I will write your name across the ballot.

You have won me over
even before the voting began.

Congratulations!

JAMES LOVE

I live such a life
not because I wanted people
to remember who I am.

                                                I live in such a way
                                                    so that people
                                                      will remember
                                          who they really are.

LOVER OF LIFE

I am a full-time lover of life.
I make love in everything I do.

Call me.

But wait, there's more!

If you smile now,
this unlimited offer is yours
absolutely free.

STARDOM

World fame is not among my fascinations.
I'd like to remain anonymous
as I possibly can.
But if it leads me down to loving you,
then I will walk the path to stardom.

I will sing, dance, and perform any act
until I become your superstar.

THE HEART OF IMAGINATION

Imagine a world
where the naive one stares
at the dancer moving her body
to the hymn of the musician's flute.

The dancer stops to gaze
as the painter paints the sky
into his heart-canvas
until the brushes break.

He will lend the broken piece of wood
to the carpenter who builds houses
for the wandering souls.

When each play ends,
every artist will go home
and return to naiveness.

In their silence,
The poet will whisper phrases
alchemizing love into living art
that sets the world
beyond imagination.

THE MANUSCRIPT

From the instant of knowing you,
I began writing love letters to myself.

Enclosed are the pages
of the greatest story untold.

····

But here's a secret invitation
I am sending you.

Open your heart.

The original manuscript
is written there.

CHANGE TOPIC

Very well,
let's drop all these nonsense talks
and discuss something else.

Something of my keen interest.

Like love.

Like us.

HI

By the way,
Poetry, this is the girl
you've been written about.

Say *Hi*.

                              Honey, meet the poem
                    that made the four-letter word
                        fall out from the writer
                          who has fallen for you.

                                      Say *Hello*.

THE MASTERPIECE

My language is not that eloquent.
My style, not so classy.
But if your body were a stripped canvas,
my loving service will be guaranteed.

I will draw each letter,
syllable by syllable,
word after word after word
with a mouthful of passionate strokes,
one coating on top of another.

And just when you're about
to lose your breath,
I will mark every punctuation with a kiss
so tender that leaves
a lasting dent on your soul.

Brace yourself my love.
This is a piece of solemn poetry
I will never get tired of writing.

YOUR BOOK

Can you do me a favor?
Stop smiling at me please.
I'm planning to write something
about misery and loneliness here.
You are ruining my plan.

For your information,
you have unknowingly invaded my privacy.
Your name has been written
all over the pages of my diary.

Define love, your face gave it definition.
The sound of your voice, my motto.
Your heart, my permanent address.

This book was supposedly
about my life story.

It is slowly becoming
your autobiography.

OMNIPRESENCE

You can never be in two places
at the same time.

In that case,
I need you to be completely honest with me.

How can you be wherever you are
and be running in circles in my mind
at the same time,
all the time?

Are you some kind of an angel
or something?

WINGS

When I walk with you,
each step we take
defies the laws of gravity.

Honey, hold on to me.
With your hand in mine,
walking is the last thing on my mind.

                              Let's fly!

DANCE

It's the music of life.

You can't see what you hear.
But there's something in it
that makes you tap your feet.

The beat invites you to dance.
And without making a move,
you smile.
Because you felt
the dancer in you came alive.

You nod your head.
You snap your fingers.
And again, you tap your feet.
One on the right, two on the left.
Without measure, they move
in harmony with each other.

It's the song I came here
to dance to.
May I, with you?

I LOVE YOU TOO, SUN

The Sun rises on one side
                        as it sets in on the other.

No matter which side you look at,
                        love remains the same.

                Beautiful.

Here,

                                there,

                and everywhere.

MEDI-DATE

According to my spiritual teacher,
my life will change
if I practice evening meditation
and focus all of my undivided attention
to something eternally beautiful.

So, I hope you wouldn't mind me asking.

But would you,

by any chance,

be free tonight?

THE ANSWER

You are more than apple to my eye.
For you, among the many things I've seen,
are what made the nights more splendid.
You hung the moon in my sky.

Is it you that revolves around my world?
Or is it me dancing around yours?

Oh, how I love the mystery.
One question leads to another,
pulling me closer and closer.
Every time I ask,
you are the every answer.

LAST JUDGEMENT

                Your conscience found me guilty
                    for our secret love affair.
                        In stealing your heart,
                  I was the prime accessory.

      I killed every reason that stood in our way
      and burned down thoughts that separate us.

You still feel the burning, don't you?

                    Your honor, if loving you is a crime,
        I'm afraid I will be your most wanted criminal.
        In all the worlds, I will be notorious for being so.

                No one can imprison me!

                          Unless, of course,
                you are the arresting officer.

For to be held in your hands
I will renounce my rights.
To you, and in you alone,
I willingly surrender.

So take me away,
                then sentence me to eternal life
                                  in love.

HEAVEN ON EARTH

Stay still.

                                            Just breathe.

I'm going to study the strands of your hair
and the curl of your eyelashes.

                              I figured I won't be seeing your soul
                                        anytime soon.

But this human garment you wear
will do.

                          Seeing your presence on earth
                is reasonable enough for me to believe

                                    that heaven
                                          is

                                        for real.

EARTH OF MINE

You are my Earth.
And I want to love you
as if you were the only planet
that exists in my Universe.

THE TOURIST

I made plans of taking a tour in your world.
You happen to be my favorite destination!

Guide me.
I wish to have my first stop at your fingertips,
take a walk from there,
           then go to every corner,
slide to your every curve
           until we land at the center of attraction.

                          Your heart.

Let's stay there for a little while.
           You see, I've been to many spectacles.
           Your beauty is the single mystery
           I want to unravel.

You can leave me there.
I would love to stay a little longer and wait
           until the most magical moment arrives.

                          Your smile.

Before we depart,
I will send kisses to your ears whispering,

                      "Oh God, I love this place.
                          Best vacation ever."

HAPPY BIRTHDAY

Mother often said
I was born to love the world.

I have come of right age
but still I linger
in doubt and bewilderment.

Then you came along,
and the world was made flesh.

Suddenly,
I heard trumpets
being sounded from the heavens
and the choir of angels joyously exclaiming,

"Happy birthday!"

HONEYLOVE

I was thinking of the fondest term
of endearment to call you.

Thanks to poetry,
I came up with a myriad different ways
to spell your name.

HALLELUJAH

        There is an insatiable longing within me.
              A fire consuming my senses,
        leading me to the edge of my sanity.
            This is a blissful alchemy
       transforming desires into worship.

Oh honey,
I long to spend the rest of my days
making every moment with you
like a thanksgiving prayer.

              Your body will be my temple
                  and I will meditate only
              on the sound of your breath.

Love will be our living testament.
Our lives will preach
an exchange of glorious praises
and chants of resounding hallelujahs!

HEARTNAPPED

Excuse me officer,
I want to report someone
who took something that belongs to me.

"Can you describe this someone elaborately?"

Oh, how can I forget?
Her eyes contain the magical essence
that holds the Universe in its grandeur.
She treads the Earth with such grace,
I watched as time stood still.

She has this way of drawing
the finest line on her lips,
carries along serenity with it.
She seduces with deceiving wits
to which any lover will pleasingly yield.

Her body is clothed with exquisite beauty.
Her voice, armed with alluring certainty.
She laughs, as if she could live forever.
Indeed, she lives in me now evermore.

"And what exactly did she steal from you?"

Something that always belongs to her.
My heart.

DAILY REMINDER

While you were away,
I developed a habit of loving myself.
This is how I learned the recipe
for unconditional love.

Have no worry about returning the favor.
I will take whatever you can offer,
not asking for more than what you can give.

You are enough.

But if you insist,
you can leave your kiss mark
on my cheek every morning
and write me daily notes
as a reminder that you,
who used to be my fondest dream,
are now the sweetest bit of my reality.

FAIRYTALE

I understand.
It's not that easy to follow
your heart's desire.

So when people come to ask me
if the journey to the unknown
was worth all the risks,
I simply tell them how
all uncertainties became certain
when I found you.

They never believe in fairytales.
But it gave them hope
for a dream worth believing.

DREAMS

Dear Dreamer,

> How far have you got to go
> before you choose to pursue me?
>
> How much waiting will I have to endure
> before you take a chance?
> The chance I faintly ask of you.
>
> Not once did I stop believing.
> And I will come to you
> the moment you start to believe.
>
> For something that you love doing,
> I am worth all the risks.
> As sure as the glory in heaven,
> I am even more than worthy.
>
> Please don't give up on me.

We are never too late,

Your Dreams

TRUTH

YOUR HOME IS IN YOUR HEART

Open your doors.
Welcome all visitors.
Fear, Anger, Grief, and their relatives,
let them in.

Greet them with a smile.
Ask where did they come from,
and what stories they bring.
Listen.
They will get tired speaking.

When they become hungry,
do not feed them.
When they become thirsty,
pour them wine until they're drunk.
Give them a hug and whisper,
"You've come to the wrong place.
Go and Peace be with you."

Breathe. Today is through.
Sleep.
Tomorrow is the beginning of your journey.
Darkness awaits outside.
Carry the light and keep it burning.
Every wanderer you meet
is searching for a star.
Be the Sun and shine without asking.

Then, keep walking.

Once in a while, be still.
Look around and witness every miracle.

If in your path you lose sight,
close your eyes
and you will remember your way back home.

LIFE'S A FRIEND

If you befriend fear,
what else is there to be afraid of?

If you befriend pain,
what else is there to suffer from?

If you befriend the past,
what else is there to regret about?

If you befriend your enemy,
who else is there to fight?

> My friend, life is not a battle.

>> If there is no more fighting,
>> all that is left is the beauty
>> that remains to be seen.

>> Love.

GRATITUDE

Right here, right now,
at this very moment,

I am grateful
>not for the music I am hearing,
>but for the gift of hearing the music.

I am grateful
>not for the words I am speaking,
>but for the gift of speaking the words.

I am grateful
>not for the emotion I am feeling,
>but for the gift of feeling the emotion.

>   In love.
I am grateful because I am.

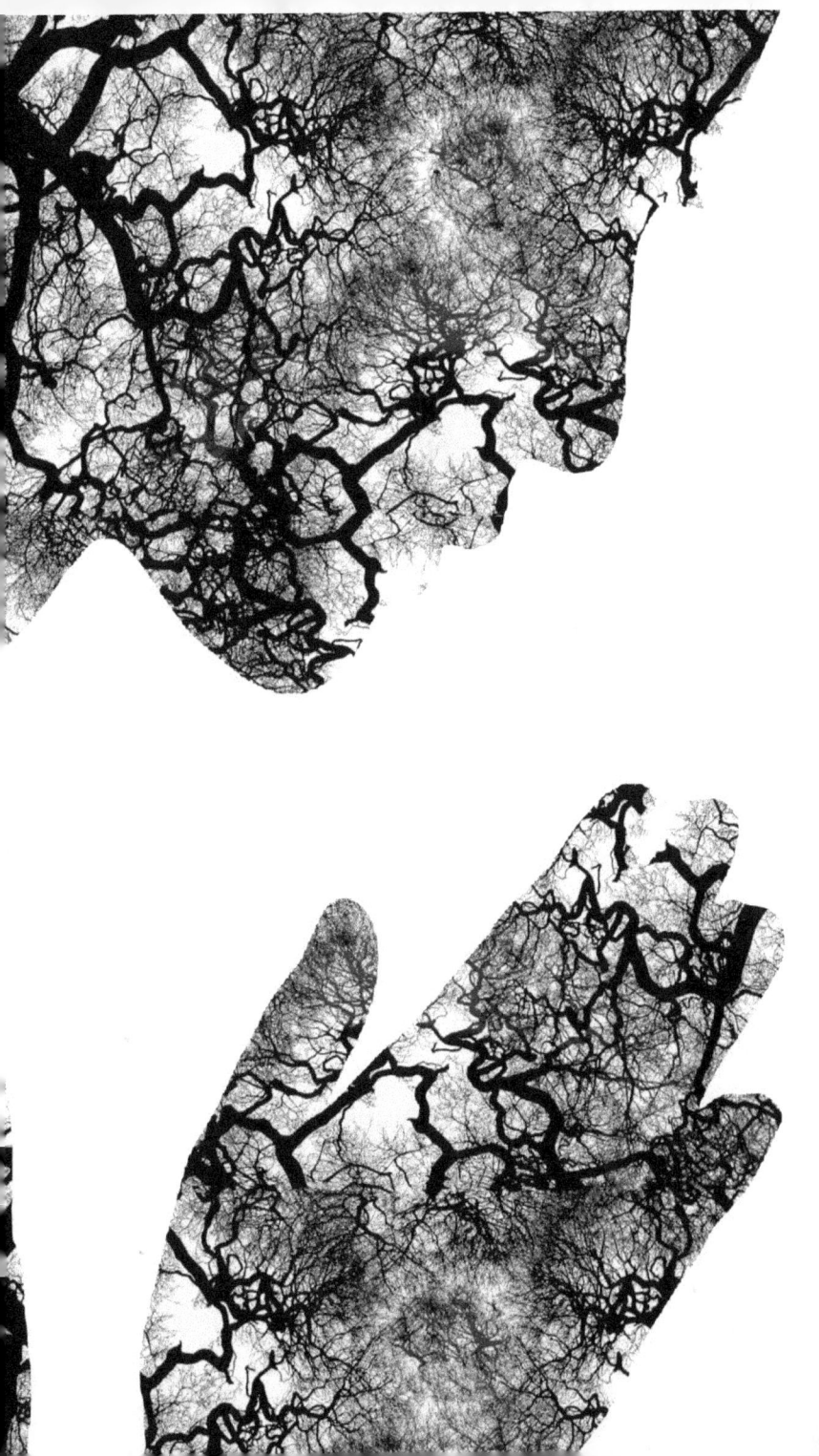

THE VOICE

The world speaks many languages.
I find them hard to understand.
But ever since I heard your voice,
all I wanted to do is listen.

PURPOSE

Maybe what the world really needs is love
more than anything.
For us to love it
in every possible way we can.
If each and every one
has that kind of purpose in life,
then we have done
more than what
it could ever ask for.

FREE WILL

                              Life has two choices.
                                      One is fear,
                                  the other, love.

We came here out of love.
But we grew in fear.

Love is who we are.
Fear taught us we were someone else.

War and suffering are outcomes of fear.
Peace and happiness are fruits of love.

                                      Fear is the disease.
                                            Love heals.

                                      Fear is the illusion.
                                      Love is the reality.

                                         Fear knows death.
                                         Love is immortal.

                                      Fear separates us.
                                     Love makes us whole.

Fear favors the right and blames the wrong.
Love holds no judgment.
It is the only Truth.

Fear is bounded by rules.
Love is self-governed.

Fear imprisons us.
Love sets us free.

Fear is the absence of Love.
Love is the absence of fear.

Life is the result of the choice we make.
Imagine what it could be
if only we were not afraid.

SCREAM

> Unspoken words are the loudest.
> For the heart feels
> what the ears cannot hear.
> And the eyes speak
> what the tongue cannot say.

When love finally breaks its silence,
let us become its voice.

> Let's sing the song of our souls.
> I am your verses.
> You, my melody.

FREEDOM

All rules, beliefs, dogmas and standards
can be summarized in one word: fear.

Do you realize now
how fear manipulates the world?

Humans became their own prisoner
within the walls they have built around themselves.

Fear needs love, not rules.

And when love finally rules over the world,
humans
        will then
                ultimately attain

                      f r e e d o m.

PATIENCE

I wait for the day
when the poor become rich
and the rich become poor.

I will wait
until they come to realize that
without love,
you can gain anything
but still never have enough.
With love,
you can lose anything
but still have everything.

HEALING

Healing is a journey.

It's not always about the destination,
but the whole experience.

It's about the people you meet,
how their stories touched your life
and how yours touched theirs.

> And in the end,
> what's going to matter most
> is not how you made yourself better,
> but how the world became a better place
> through you.

POSITIVE

Affirmations are like sowing seeds.

Remember the parable?
Be a fertile soil.
Your mind is your garden
and you are the gardener.

Keep cultivating positive thoughts.
When you plant today,
don't dig out the crop tomorrow.

There's a right time for harvest.
Water them with gratitude everyday.

Sooner than you thought,
and usually when you least expect it,
you start harvesting a bounty of miracles.

And before you know it,
your garden has already grown
into an abundant forest.

INNOCENCE

Let the children be children.

The child knows better than you do.
If you think so otherwise, think again.

The child knows the Truth in their hearts.
You hold nothing but beliefs in your minds.

I came here not to convince you of the Truth,
but rather to question your beliefs.

What happened to that child
who pretends to be a man or a woman?

Return to your innocence.
Let the child be child again.
Wake from your dream
and let the child in you awaken!

THE SCIENTIST

There is a place we meet
that is not a where.

Love said to me,
"Come, I'll take you to Paradise."

Reason cannot follow us
and logic can do nothing but wonder,
"How can one plus one equals one?
You must be out of your mind!
I therefore conclude,
you must have found it.
Eureka!"

TRUE LOVE

Where there is love, there is no need.
Where there is need, there is suffering.

Do not mistake need for love.
Need imprisons.
Love liberates.
'I need you' means suffering.
'I love you' entails freedom.

Imagine being loved by someone
without needing you.
That is True Love.

True Love can only be found within.

A True Lover seeks himself first.
Once found, he needs nothing else.
Because he has no need,
he gives everything of himself.
He doesn't complete someone by filling a need.
He does love someone
by loving someone completely.

Imagine being a True Lover to someone.
That is falling in love.

A love with no need.
Just love.

CHANGELESS

>Wandering from places to places,
>I return to where I've always been.
>Funny, I remember the place
>but no longer myself.

Who I am is not who I was,
neither who I will be.
Though I wear many faces,
I am changeless.
Change is merely a thing I do.

>Dying to be alive.
>Living to be free.

There is somewhere I'd like you to see.
If you wish to know the truth of who you are,
follow the voice that calls you home.

>Go there.
>For where our love is,
>there we will be.

HAPPINESS

I am happy.

I choose myself to be.

Then Happiness,
having heard its name,
came looking for me
to show a thousand reasons
why I am.

LASTING BEAUTY

We cannot behold the elegance of a rose
by merely looking at its petals
without honoring its thorns.

True lasting beauty emerges
from the deepest wounds.
It's the ugliest scar
that makes the beauty last.

KINDNESS

Kindness is a sure quickest way to get rich.

In this business,
everyone will be your customer.

Wherever you go,
there is a marketplace.

> Believe me,
> this is the real deal.

> Invest now!

GAME

There are no rules. Have fun!

Never mind the crowd watching you.
Whatever you hear is irrelevant.
Be responsible for the thoughts
running in your mind.
That is your territory.
Own it!

Laugh when you stumble.
Remember, this is part of your strategy.
Critics would ask, *"Why play if not for winning?"*
They are the ones who never learn enjoyment
and never enjoy learning;
Obsessed with the results,
but not committed to the process.

In every round,
have the eagerness of a rookie
and the temerity of a champion.
As long as you're trying to win,
you're going to lose.

The real game commences when you
are no longer attached to the outcome.

Until then,
keep practicing.

TREASURE OF THE HEART

The riches of this world
can never compare
to the treasure of the Universe
inside you.
Seek that.

Do what you love.

And you will find the light
that leads to your heart.

HIDE AND SEEK

Don't look for me
at the corners of your mind
for you will not see me there.

Search within
the depths of your heart
and you will find
that I was there all along.

WORDS

A knife can cut through bones.
In time, the flesh will heal itself.
But words are the finest
double-edged samurai
swiftly inflicting wounds on the soul
of both the oppressed
and the oppressor.

The rage will come to end,
but the search for cure
will last for eternity.

SELF-MASTERY

Never use your own pain to hurt others.
That is the lamest display of cowardice,
the weakest form of fear.

If you want to know
what true bravery is,
go to your room, alone with yourself.
There you will find your enemy.

Do not get out until you befriended it.
Your friendship will form a mighty alliance.
Therein awaits your greatest conquest.
Victory comes after the surrender.

When you have truly mastered yourself,
I promise,
you will never taste defeat
ever again.

WARRIOR OF THE LIGHT

I will never ask
that you understand my battles.

I can only hope
that in my return,
you will be strong enough
to see my wounds.

LOVE AND LIGHT

We rise, we fall.
Love sees through it all.

A candle lights up a room
when it's willing to see its smoke.
A firework ignites the sky
because it chooses to hear its noise.

We cannot reveal our radiance
without casting our shadows.

I had to face her demons
to feel the feathers of her wings.
As I offered her roses,
she also accepted my thorns.

Love is about searching for light in darkness.

In darkness, I found myself in her.

In light, she found herself in me.

SOUL TO SOUL

Love someone with your body,
you have him for a night.

Love someone with your heart,
you have her for a lifetime.

Love someone with your soul,
you have each other for eternity.

"Oh darling,
you have my mind confused!"
said the lover.
"Tell me, when do I begin
the love that has no ending?"

The beloved replied,
"Why ask a question of time
to a timeless answer?
Love me now
and I'm yours forever."

STANDBY

I want the love that speaks through silence.
The love that doesn't need
to prove anything to anyone
because it can stand for itself.

>   Like the way we stand together
>   side by side.
>   And even in that standing alone,
>   doing nothing,
>   we stand for everything.

Love stands.
Then you and I just follow its lead.

FISH IN THE OCEAN

You've become my sacred obsession.
The divinity in me yearns for your humanness.
I long to discover the rest of who I am
by exploring every aspect of who you are.

> Do not be contented with anything
> less than what you deserve.
> Never settle for anybody
> less than what you can be.

Fools say there are many fishes in the sea.
Yet they can never seem to fathom
that in my innermost depths,

> far beyond
> any other creature's reach,

where all raging waters
   find tranquility,

> you

> are the only one

> dwelling

> in my ocean.

SOMEONE SOMEWHERE

                        A stranger by day,
                    I was told not to let you in.
                  In my longing to know you,
                      I asked for your name.

You spelled it with a knife
that pierced through my heart.
This pain in my chest
sees beauty in your eyes.

                    Tear me apart for your view.
                Open the window of my wounds.
                    To catch one glimpse of you
                    is worth a thousand cures.

A thief in the night,
you stole a kiss that awakens.
I was brought to life,
yet you left me breathless.

                    I did not sense you coming in.
                      For there is a silence
                      even the deaf can hear.
                          There is a beauty
                      even the blind can see.
                          There is a touch
                    even the numb can feel.

Speak to me now quietly
the sound that makes the trees sway.
Whisper to my ears
the song that birds sing.

                              The world casts a spell.
                    We are trapped in this illusion.
                          Shed me your light.
                        And unveil what is real.

Tonight, meet me in between.
Today, I'm nearer than a heartbeat.

                        If breath is as close as I can get,
                        tomorrow, I'll become the wind
                            just to be with you again.

CHALLENGE

> Fear called me impossible,
> I accomplished.

> Death threatened my end,
> I conquered.

> Guilt enslaved my freedom,
> I redeemed.

For the final challenge,
ego dared me
not to fall in love with you.

> I caught your smile.

> With my heart leaping in ecstasy,
> I heard its call for sweet surrender.

> As effortless as that,
> I did.

CHANGE

You may not be able to change the world
with what you do.
But you can make a difference
with who you are.

Doing means nothing.
Being is everything.
So strive to be the one
who does endless becoming.

Be the Forgiveness
that blame cannot give.

Be the Gratitude
that lack takes for granted.

Be the Compassion
that indifference cannot feel.

Be the Tolerance
that anger cannot understand.

Be the Truth in a place buried
under deception and lies.
Make all beliefs questionable,
so they will remember
what is only worth remembering.

Be that and more.
Embody your limitlessness.

But first and above all,
be Love.
The Love that everyone has spoken about,
but no one has ever heard of.

                        Be you.

                    That, my friend,
                      is the change
                  you want to become
                      in the world.

MOTHER AND CHILD

Mother once told me,
"*You are free
to live the life you love.
Go, be the greatest expression
and the grandest experience of all that you are.*"

I understood everything except for one,
so I asked,
"*Mother, can I also choose who to love?*"

To which She graciously answered,
"*My dear child,
it is love that chooses you.*

*You will be facing two choices by then.
You choose yourself, or
you choose love.*

*The world believes you have to
sacrifice one for the other.*

*Only those few
who dare to seek what is true
will love the life they live.*

And they are those who choose both."

TWIN FLAME

Separate but one.
Broken but whole.
This is where I find solitude.

> You are because I am.
> I am because you are.
> This is where I find solace.

>> You are asleep.
>> I am awake.
>> We are lost in a dream.
>> This is the place where we meet.

THE VOW

I no longer know death.
What we have can surpass anything.
You distill my doubts.
You destroy my fears.
You know my secrets that even I
have kept hidden from myself.
Yet you bear them like they are yours to keep.
My vulnerability feels adorable in your sight.
My weaknesses feel safe in your embrace.

My writings overspill
with words of an ardent lover.
The strings of verses
became more intimate with each other.
What used to end with question marks
are now never-ending declarations
of lovely vows.

Every little thing makes perfect sense.
Even my smallest act has meaning.
My simplest gesture has purpose.
All that and more simply because
of you being here.

So let me thank you.
I intend to make up for all the times
we've been apart.

Forever with you is my goal
and you here with me
is where I begin.

I've always loved poetry.
I remember now.

www.ingramcontent.com/pod-product-compliance
Lightning Source LLC
Chambersburg PA
CBHW061329040426
42444CB00011B/2834